OCEANS AND SEAS

CARIBBEAN SEA AND GULF OF MEXICO

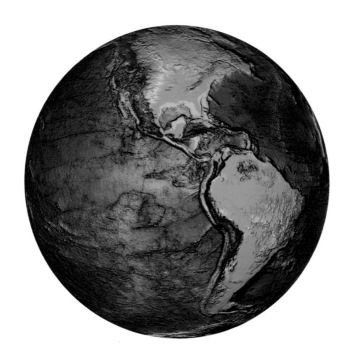

by Jen Green

WORLD ALMANAC® LIBRARY

Please visit our web site at: www.worldalmanaclibrary.com
For a free color catalog describing World Almanac® Library's list of
high-quality books and multimedia programs, call 1-800-848-2928 (USA)
or 1-800-387-3178 (Canada). World Almanac® Library's fax: (414) 332-3567.

Library of Congress Cataloging-in-Publication Data

Green, Jen.
    Caribbean Sea and Gulf of Mexico / Jen Green.
        p. cm. — (Oceans and seas)
    Includes bibliographical references and index.
    ISBN 0-8368-6272-4 (lib. bdg.)
    ISBN 0-8368-6280-5 (softcover)
        1. Caribbean Sea—Juvenile literature.   2. Mexico, Gulf of—Juvenile literature.   I. Title.
    GC531.G74   2006
    551.46'1365—dc22   2005054137

First published in 2006 by
World Almanac® Library
A Member of the WRC Media Family of Companies
330 West Olive Street, Suite 100
Milwaukee, WI 53212 USA

Copyright © 2006 by World Almanac® Library.

Produced by Discovery Books
Editor: Sabrina Crewe
Designer and page production: Sabine Beaupré
Photo researcher: Sabrina Crewe
Maps and diagrams: Stefan Chabluk
Geographical consultant: Keith Lye
World Almanac® Library editorial direction: Valerie Weber
World Almanac® Library editor: Gini Holland
World Almanac® Library art direction: Tammy West
World Almanac® Library graphic design: Charlie Dahl
World Almanac® Library production: Jessica Morris and Robert Kraus

Picture credits: Corbis: cover, pp. 9, 33, 35; FEMA: p. 19 (top, bottom); FLPA: pp. 25
(right), 26, 27, 42; Getty Images: pp. 16, 23 (top), 25 (left), 30, 32, 39 (top), 40; NASA:
p. 8; NOAA: pp. 6, 11 (both), 12 (both), 13, 18 (both), 19 (middle), 20, 21 (all), 23 (middle,
bottom), 24 (both), 29, 31, 36 (both), 37, 38, 39 (bottom), 41; NOAA/NGDC: title page.

Printed in the United States of America

1 2 3 4 5 6 7 8 9 10 09 08 07 06

CONTENTS

Front cover: *The Caribbean Sea and Gulf of Mexico are known for their coral reefs. This colorful reef scene is in the Caribbean Sea.*
Title page: *This computer-generated image of Earth was based on land and ocean measurements made by the U.S. National Geophysical Data Center. This view shows the Gulf of Mexico and the Caribbean Sea as the areas below the southern coast of the United States and above the northern tip of South America.*

Words that appear in the glossary are printed in **boldface** the first time they occur in text.

The Caribbean Sea and **Gulf** of Mexico are two neighboring bodies of water. Both are part of the Atlantic Ocean. Edged on the west by the eastern shores of Central America, the Gulf and Caribbean are linked to each other by the Yucatán Channel between Cuba and Mexico. Together, the Caribbean Sea and Gulf of Mexico are called the "wider" or "greater" Caribbean. The two waters share **tropical** weather and much of their history. The Caribbean and Gulf are, however, different in several ways.

The Gulf of Mexico

The Gulf of Mexico covers 615,000 square miles (1,592,850 square kilometers). Roughly oval in shape, it measures about 800 miles (1,290 kilometers) from north to south and roughly 1,100 miles (1,770 km) from east to west. The long,

A Rare Gem

". . . the Caribbean Sea, one of the world's most alluring bodies of water, a rare gem among the oceans, defined by the islands that form a chain of lovely jewels to the north and east."

James A. Michener, Caribbean, *1989*

curving coastline of the United States and Mexico enclose it to the north, west, and south, with the large island of Cuba to the east. In the northeast, the **Straits** of Florida link the Gulf to the rest of the Atlantic. The Gulf of Mexico has few islands apart from western Cuba and the island chain of the Florida Keys.

The Caribbean Sea

The Caribbean Sea, in contrast, is known for its many islands. The Caribbean is much larger than the Gulf, covering 1,049,500 square miles (2,718,200 sq km). This sea is much wider than it is long, measuring about 1,500 miles (2,400 km) from east to west. Like the Gulf, the Caribbean is mostly bounded by land—to the west lie Mexico and most of Central America, while Panama, Colombia, and Venezuela lie to the south. The islands of the Greater Antilles form the northern boundary. To the east, the Lesser Antilles curve from the Virgin Islands to the coast of Venezuela. The Caribbean is named after the Carib people who settled its islands long ago.

Many Resources

The Gulf of Mexico and Caribbean have very different natural resources. This fact

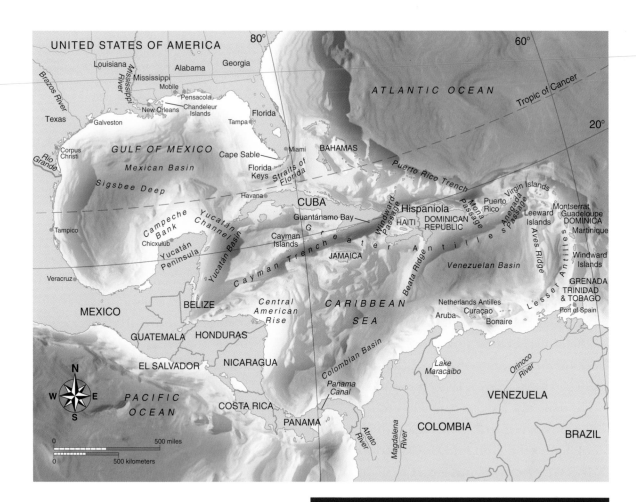

This map shows the Gulf of Mexico and the Caribbean Sea, their major islands and underwater features, and the landmasses that border them.

has caused their coasts, islands, and waters to be developed in separate ways. Tourism is the main industry in the Caribbean, where the sunny climate, warm seas, coral **reefs**, and fine beaches attract millions of visitors each year. The Gulf of Mexico also has fine beaches, but it is rich in natural resources that include fish as well as oil and other **minerals**. Long stretches of the Gulf coastline are now developed with factories and oil refineries.

Gulf of Mexico and Caribbean Sea Key Facts

Gulf of Mexico surface area: 615,000 square miles (1,592,850 sq km)
Gulf of Mexico deepest known point: 17,070 feet (5,203 meters), Sigsbee Deep
Caribbean Sea surface area: 1,049,500 square miles (2,718,200 sq km)
Caribbean Sea deepest known point: 25,216 feet (7,686 m) in the Cayman Trench between Jamaica and the Cayman Islands

CHAPTER ONE

PHYSICAL FEATURES

As in other seas and oceans, the floors of the Caribbean and Gulf of Mexico are not flat. Beneath the surface lie craggy mountains and **ridges**, gently sloping rises, curving basins, and deep trenches.

Scientists believe that these features were formed by movements of the giant, rigid sections—known as tectonic plates—that make up Earth's outer layers. Three main tectonic plates are thought to lie below the Gulf and Caribbean: the North American, South American, and Caribbean plates. The movements of these plates and other factors ensure that the Gulf of Mexico and the Caribbean Sea are still changing today.

Formation

Earth's tectonic plates have been in motion ever since the planet's outer layers solidified. Some geologists believe that the Caribbean and Gulf of Mexico began to form as early as 300 million years ago. They believe that at this time, during the Paleozoic era, the area that is now the Caribbean Sea lay close to what is today the Mediterranean Sea. Some 110 million years ago, molten rock began welling up along what is now the Mid-Atlantic Ridge. This movement separated the Eurasian and North American Plates, and a great basin gradually formed between them. It filled with water to become the Atlantic Ocean, with the Mediterreranean in the east and the Caribbean in the west. Other scientists have a

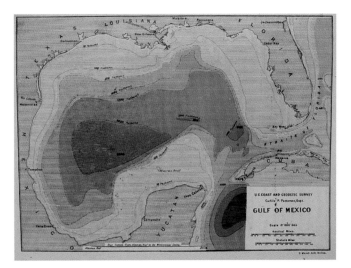

The floors of the world's oceans and seas were a total mystery until the 1870s. Then, using more than three thousand deepwater soundings, U.S. scientists were able to produce this chart showing the different depths of the Gulf of Mexico. It was the first realistic map of any oceanic basin. The varying shades of blue indicate different depths, with the darkest areas being the deepest.

Plates and Oceans

Earth's outer layers are made up of a number of vast, rigid sections called tectonic plates—seven major ones and up to twelve smaller ones. Fitting together like pieces of a jigsaw puzzle, the plates underlie oceans and dry land. The plates drift across Earth's surface, floating on a lower, molten layer of the **mantle** like chunks of bread on a thick, bubbling soup. As they drift, tectonic plates can push together, grind past one another, or pull apart.

Volcanic eruptions and earthquakes are common along plate boundaries because the crust is thinnest there. Where two plates pull apart, as is happening in the center of the Atlantic, **magma** rises to fill the space, creating a mountain chain underwater or on land. Elsewhere, plates collide. Where this happens, one plate may dive below the other to form a deep trench, such as the Cayman Trench (in the Caribbean Sea) and the Puerto Rico Trench (where the Caribbean meets the wider Atlantic Ocean).

About 250 million years ago, Earth's landmasses were united in a single "super-continent" named Pangaea, which was surrounded by a vast ocean now known as Panthalassa. About 200 million years ago, because of **continental drift** caused by plate movement, a great bay—the Tethys Sea—opened up in the center of Pangaea and split it in half. The northern landmass—named Laurasia—included North America, Greenland, Europe, and Asia, while the southern half—Gondwanaland—included South America, Africa, India, Australia, and Antarctica. As plate movement continued over millions of years, the continents and oceans took their present positions (shown below, with the major tectonic plates), and they continue to shift today.

different opinion. They believe the Caribbean was once part of the Pacific, but became separated from it by the landmass of Central America, which rose and drifted to its present site. (It was not entirely separated, because at this time Central America was not yet joined to South America.)

Scientists believe that the Gulf of Mexico formed as part of the North American plate subsided. Deposits in the Gulf of minerals named **evaporites**, which form when large quantities of seawater **evaporate**, suggest that it was once much shallower than it is today.

A Meteorite in the Gulf

About 65 million years ago, the southern coastline of the Gulf of Mexico was reshaped by entirely different force: the crash landing of an enormous **meteorite**. This meteorite is thought to have been

Chicxulub Crater

The meteorite that that landed near Chicxulub in the late Cretaceaous period, about 65 million years ago, was an estimated 6 miles (10 km) in diameter. The crater left by the meteorite, a large circle stretching under both land and sea, measures over 112 miles (180 km) across. (There may be an outer ring that is even larger.) A crash of this size would have raised giant waves, or tsunamis, and an enormous cloud of dust that would have covered Earth's surface and blotted out the Sun for many years. Some scientists believe this event and the resulting climate change were responsible for the extinction of dinosaurs, marine **mollusks** called ammonites, and many other species that all died out at that time. Recent discoveries indicate that the Chicxulub meteorite may have been one of several that hit Earth in the same period—

smaller craters of a similar age have been discovered in Britain and in Ukraine. The image of the Chicxulub crater above is a **radar** image produced by NASA that shows a curving line, part of a circle, on the northwest tip of the Yucatán Peninsula around Chicxulub. The line forms the rim of the now-buried crater on land—it is in fact a trough about 3 miles (5 km) wide and 10–15 feet (3–4.6 m) deep. The rest of the crater's rim lies underwater in the Gulf of Mexico.

one of the largest ever to strike Earth. The crater left by the huge chunk of rock lies mostly offshore, with its center in the Gulf of Mexico near the town of Chicxulub on the Yucatán **Peninsula**.

Later Plate Movements

As recently as 3.5 million years ago, the Caribbean took its present shape as plate movements forced a narrow neck of land, the **isthmus** of Panama, to rise upward, linking North and South America. Before this, the Caribbean had been open to the Pacific.

Plate movements in the region continue today. They are affected by upheaval far to the east, in the center of the wider Atlantic. There, the seafloor is spreading and causing the North American and South American Plates to drift slowly westward. The Caribbean Plate, meanwhile, is being forced eastward. The resulting collision has caused large trenches to appear in some areas. Elsewhere, undersea ridges have risen as the seafloor is crumpled between plates. This upheaval also causes frequent earthquakes and volcanic eruptions. Earthquakes are caused by sudden shifts along breaks in Earth's crust, while most volcanoes occur when magma wells up along or near tectonic plate borders.

Features of the Gulf Floor

The floor of the Gulf of Mexico is shallow and relatively smooth compared to the Caribbean. The bed of the Gulf is

An image taken from the Space Shuttle shows how the isthmus of Panama narrowly separates the Caribbean Sea (top right) *from the Pacific Ocean* (bottom left).

shaped like a enormous shallow basin. The basin has a wide rim formed by continental shelves—ledges of gently sloping land extending out from the mainland, where the water is less than 660 feet (200 m) deep. The continental shelves of the Gulf are between 25 miles and 200 miles (40 km and 320 km) wide. The Campeche Bank off the Yucatán Peninsula is one of the widest areas.

The continental shelves and coastal shallows of the Gulf make up 80 percent of the seafloor, leaving just 20 percent occupied by waters more than 9,800 feet (3,000 m) deep. The deepest point in the Gulf of Mexico, Sigsbee Deep, is 17,070 feet (5,203 m) below the surface and lies in the west. A thick layer of salty deposits covers large areas of the seafloor. In places, this layer has been forced upward to form rises called salt domes. Deposits of oil and gas are often found near the salt domes. Elsewhere, thick deposits of limestone, sand, or clay cover the floor of the Gulf.

The Caribbean Seafloor

The floor of the Caribbean is much deeper than the Gulf, with large areas more than 12,000 feet (3,660 m) deep. The deepest waters of these basins can plunge to 16,500 feet (5,030 m) or more—as deep as some other Atlantic basins. The floor of the Caribbean Sea is extremely uneven. Much of it is covered by deposits of red clay or the remains of microscopic plants and animals that have drifted down from above.

There are four main basins, divided from each other by undersea ridges or rises. From west to east, these are the Yucatán, Colombian, and Venezuelan Basins and the Cayman Trench (also called the Cayman Trough or Cayman Basin). The sea's deepest point—25,216 feet (7,686 m) below the surface—is located in the Cayman Trench. Such trenches form where two oceanic plates collide and one is forced below the other.

Islands of the Caribbean

Large numbers of islands dot the Caribbean and separate it from the rest of the Atlantic. They range in size from large, mountainous masses, such as Cuba and Hispaniola, to small, low-lying islands just a few miles across. In the west, Cuba, Jamaica, Hispaniola, and Puerto Rico are the largest of the Greater Antilles. In the east, a chain of smaller islands, the Lesser Antilles, runs from the Virgin Islands south to the coast of Venezuela. The word *Antilles* comes from Antilia, a mythical island chain that sailors long ago believed lay in the west Atlantic. The Caribbean islands are sometimes called the West Indies.

This diagram shows some of the features that form on Earth's sea and ocean floors.

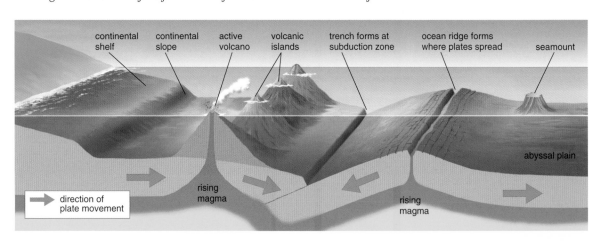

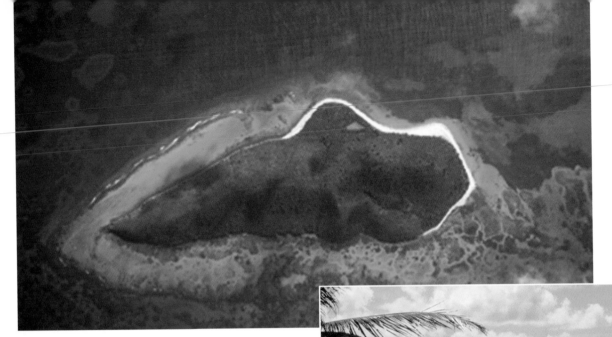

Two-thirds of the tiny Buck Island in the U.S. Virgin Islands (above) is surrounded by a coral reef. The reef is home to many wildlife species. Islands in the Caribbean often have deep, curved bays, such as Man-of-War Bay (right) in Tobago.

Volcanic Islands

The Greater Antilles formed millions of years ago as the seafloor buckled upward between colliding plates. Many of the Lesser Antilles were formed by volcanic eruptions over the last five million years. Northeast of the Antilles, the Puerto Rico Trench marks a boundary between the North American, South American, and Caribbean Plates. A part of the South American Plate is being forced down below the Caribbean Plate along this **subduction zone**. Deep underground, the crust there has melted, and magma has surged up to form a line of volcanoes on the seafloor. The rock built up on the seabed has risen above the water's surface to form an arc of islands that includes Montserrat, Guadeloupe, Martinique, and St. Vincent.

Volcanic islands, such as Montserrat and Martinique, are mostly made of **igneous** rocks, such as basalt. Other Caribbean islands, such as Barbados, are made of limestone, a sedimentary rock. Sedimentary rocks form when layers of sand, clay, or other **sediment** get buried below other layers and are compressed to form hard rock. Yet other islands, such as the low-lying Cayman Islands, are made of sandy deposits dropped by **currents** and tides.

Volcanoes in Recent Times

Volcanic activity has continued in the region into modern times. In 1902,

Mount Pelée on Martinique exploded in a violent eruption, and a cloud of hot ash and poisonous gas engulfed the port of St. Pierre. More than thirty thousand people died—all but one of the town's inhabitants, a prisoner who was protected by the thick walls of his jail cell.

In 1995, the Soufrière Hills volcano on Montserrat began to erupt. A tide of ash, mud, and lava buried the capital, Plymouth, and the whole island had to be evacuated. The eruption rumbled on for several years. The seabed is also volcanically active. In 2001, a volcano named Kick-'em-Jenny erupted in the Caribbean Sea off the island of Grenada.

Coastlines in the Gulf and Caribbean

The sweeping coastline of the Gulf of Mexico stretches for over 3,500 miles (5,630 km), from Cape Sable in Florida to the tip of the Yucatán Peninsula. There is a further 230 miles (370 km) of Gulf coast on western Cuba. The coastline of the Caribbean, which runs from the Yucatán Peninsula through the eastern nations of Central America to Venezuela on the South American mainland and includes parts of many of the Antilles, is about twice as long.

Many coasts of the region are low-lying, and therefore they lack rugged features, such as cliffs. Instead, deep inlets, sweeping beaches, **marshes**, and mangrove swamps are common there. The region's rivers carry huge amounts of sediment to the sea. The sediment is then dropped at river mouths to form wide **deltas**, such as the Mississippi Delta. Sand and sediment are also carried along the coast by currents and later dropped to form **barrier islands** with sheltered pools and marshes on the land side.

An aerial view of the Mississippi Delta shows the marshes that cover much of the delta basin.

Shaping Coastlines

The natural features found on Gulf and Caribbean coasts are shaped by two main processes: erosion and deposition. Erosion is the wearing away of the land by water, wind, and other natural forces. Deposition is the laying down of rocky materials, or deposits, often in the form of fine particles such as sand, mud, or silt.

Waves are the main force of erosion on coastlines. As they beat against the shore, they hurl sand and **shingle** against rocks to wear them away. Bands of hard rock at the water's edge are left to form jutting headlands, while soft rocks are eaten away to form deep, curving bays. In some areas, waves eat into coasts by 3 feet (1 m) or more each year, gradually shifting the shore inland. Deep inlets have cut into the Caribbean coastline in places such as Lake Maracaibo in Venezuela.

Pounding waves smash rocky fragments into sand and shingle. Coastal currents may carry these materials for miles and then deposit them to form beaches, **spits**, and the barrier islands that characterize the Gulf coast.

The Mississippi Delta, one of the world's largest deltas, covers 13,000 square miles (33,670 sq km). Sediment brought down by the river in the last seven thousand years has widened the Mississippi coastal plain by 90 miles (145 km). Levies and other efforts to control this river have cut off the flow of sediment, endangering barrier islands and the delta itself.

July 17, 2001

August 31, 2005

These photographs show Chandaleur Islands, a barrier island chain formed by deposition off the coast of Louisiana and Mississippi. The islands are very vulnerable to erosion by waves. They were the focus of a major coastal restoration project completed in 2001 (top), during which cordgrass was planted to help the islands' soil resist erosion. Four years later, however, Hurricane Katrina swept through, with devastating results (bottom). Erosion of barrier islands and coastal wetlands along the Gulf of Mexico coast means that communities have less protection when major storms hit.

CHAPTER TWO

CLIMATE AND CURRENTS

Why Is the Sea Salty?

Seawater is salty because it contains dissolved minerals, or salts, washed from the land by rivers or released underwater by volcanic eruptions or other thermal activity. The salt level in seawater is higher than in rivers because, when surface water evaporates, the dissolved salts remain in the sea and become more concentrated. The Gulf of Mexico, with 36 parts of salt per thousand parts of water, is slightly saltier than the Caribbean, with 35 to 36 parts per thousand. Experts calculate that the salt in all the seas and oceans would be enough to bury Earth's landmasses to a depth of 500 feet (152 m)! So why do seas not get increasingly salty as new minerals are added each year? Some salt is removed from the water when it is absorbed by marine life or reacts with underwater rock and eventually forms new sediment layers on the ocean floor. These processes help keep salt levels constant in seas and oceans.

The Gulf of Mexico is fed by over twenty rivers, including the Mississippi, Brazos, Alabama, Rio Grande, Grijalva, and Usumacinta. The Mississippi contributes an amazing 64 percent of all freshwater entering the Gulf. The Caribbean is fed by the Magdalena and Atrato of Colombia and by many rivers on the Greater and Lesser Antilles. The freshwater from these rivers mixes with salty seawater when it reaches the seas. The Gulf and Caribbean, therefore, both have less salty areas in coastal waters where the rivers meet the sea.

Water Temperatures in the Gulf and Caribbean

Water temperatures vary with depth, as in all seas and oceans. The bottom waters are coldest, while surface waters are considerably warmer, although temperatures vary somewhat through the year. In the Caribbean, surface temperatures range from 73 to 84° Fahrenheit (23 to 29° Celsius); they drop to 39° F (4° C) in the depths. In the Gulf, surface temperatures vary between 64 and 76° F (18 and 24° C), while bottom waters remain at about 43° F (6° C).

Moisture continually circulates between the oceans, air, and land. This never-ending process, illustrated here, is known as the water cycle.

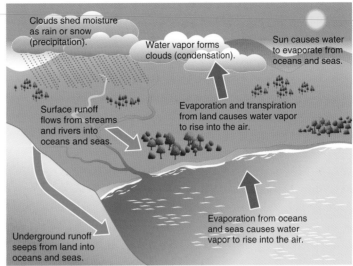

Clouds shed moisture as rain or snow (precipitation).

Water vapor forms clouds (condensation).

Sun causes water to evaporate from oceans and seas.

Surface runoff flows from streams and rivers into oceans and seas.

Evaporation and transpiration from land causes water vapor to rise into the air.

Underground runoff seeps from land into oceans and seas.

Evaporation from oceans and seas causes water vapor to rise into the air.

Trade Winds

The main winds of the region are northeasterly winds that blow southwest toward the **equator**. These are known as trade winds because they used to help trading ships sailing across the Atlantic to reach the Americas. The southern islands of the Lesser Antilles, from Dominica to Grenada, are known as the Windward Islands because they lie in the path of these favorable winds.

Caribbean and Gulf Currents

Prevailing winds drive surface currents, which flow through the seas like mighty rivers. The surface currents of the Caribbean and Gulf of Mexico flow around the coasts and islands in various directions. The water carried by the Caribbean Current heads west and north through the Caribbean, then passes

through the Yucatán Channel into the Gulf of Mexico. Some water heads east around the shores of Mexico. The rest forms the Loop Current, which makes a loop north, then south toward Florida.

This current becomes fast and strong as it passes through the Straits of Florida. Entering the wider Atlantic Ocean as the Florida Current, it is joined by the Antilles Current that flows

This map shows the most important surface currents that have been identified in the Caribbean Sea and Gulf of Mexico. Many smaller currents flow between islands and around coasts.

Gulf Stream

UNITED STATES OF AMERICA

Florida

ATLANTIC OCEAN

Antilles

Loop

GULF OF MEXICO

Straits of Florida

Mexican   Yucatán

Yucatán Channel

CUBA

Hispaniola

G r e a t e r   A n t i l l e s

Caribbean

MEXICO   BELIZE

GUATEMALA   HONDURAS

EL SALVADOR   NICARAGUA

CARIBBEAN SEA

VENEZUELA

PACIFIC OCEAN

COSTA RICA

PANAMA

COLOMBIA

BRAZIL

L e s s e r   A n t i l l e s

Heavy rains, strong winds, and waves often lash the Gulf shoreline, as shown here near Corpus Christi, Texas.

westward north of the Antilles. The currents unite to form the Gulf Stream, a warm flow of water that is one of the world's major currents. The Gulf Stream flows north, warming the eastern shores of the United States as far as Cape Hatteras in North Carolina. There, it veers northeast and heads across the wider Atlantic Ocean.

Cold bottom water circulates less freely than surface water, but there are currents in the depths as well as surface currents. Atlantic bottom water enters the Caribbean through a number of passages among the islands of the Antilles. It then sinks to become cold, dense water in the deep basins of the Caribbean Sea.

Large and Small Waves

Winds blowing across the sea whip up waves as well as surface currents. Waves more than 16 feet (5 m) high are rare in these waters except during violent storms and hurricanes. As waves move across the sea, the water in them moves around in a circle. In deep water, waves can circulate freely, but close to shore the flow is hindered by the seabed. This causes the tops of waves to break and spill over to form surf.

Towering waves called tsunamis are a threat in the region, as in all areas prone to earthquakes and volcanoes. Huge waves can radiate outward from the disturbance like ripples in a pond. In 1946, a major earthquake north of Hispaniola produced a tsunami that killed about 1,600 people in the region.

Tides in the Caribbean and Gulf

The difference between the water level at high and low tide is known as the tidal range. Both the Caribbean and the Gulf of Mexico have a fairly small tidal range. On many Caribbean islands, the water level rises and falls by just 1 foot (0.3 m). In the Bahamas, however, the tide level varies by three times that amount. On some parts of the South American coasts, the tidal range is as high as 10 feet (3 m). In most parts of the Gulf, it is less than 2 feet (0.6 m).

Climate

The Caribbean and Gulf of Mexico have a tropical or **subtropical** climate, with hot summers and warm winters. Rainfall varies greatly in the region. The island of Bonaire off Venezuela receives just 10 inches (254 millimeters) of rain in a year. To the northeast, the island of Dominica may be drenched by up 350 inches (8,890 mm) a year.

A Region of Hurricanes

The word *hurricane* comes from Huracán, the storm goddess of the Taino people. The goddess was believed to unleash the winds when she was angry. Hurricanes are a danger from June to November. These huge, spinning storms begin far out in the Atlantic, at centers of **low pressure** where warm, moist air is rising upward. As the rising air cools, its moisture **condenses**, bringing heavy rain and releasing heat that fuels the

What Causes Tides?

Tides are regular rises and falls in sea level caused mainly by the tug of the Moon's gravity. As the Moon orbits Earth, its gravity pulls ocean water into a mound below it. A similar bulge appears on the ocean on the opposite side of Earth because the planet itself is also being pulled, by the same force, away from the water on the far side. As Earth spins eastward, so the mounds move westward across Earth's surface, bringing tides to coasts in succession. Because Earth spins around once every twenty-four hours, the two bulges both move across Earth once in that period, creating two tides a day in each place. The tides are not always equal in volume, however. In some parts of more enclosed seas, such as the Gulf of Mexico, there is just one tide a day.

The Sun's gravity exerts a similar, but weaker, pull on the oceans. This is because, while many times larger than the Moon, it is also much farther away. Every two weeks, at the full moon and again during the new moon, the Sun and Moon line up so that their pulls combine. This force brings extra high tides called spring tides. They alternate with weaker tides also occurring every two weeks, named neap tides, when the two pulls tend to minimize each other.

A 2005 satellite image shows the enormous Hurricane Katrina, with the eye at its center clearly visible, over the Gulf of Mexico and heading for land.

three huge storms—Hurricanes Katrina, Rita, and Wilma—hit U.S. coasts in the busiest Atlantic season on record.

Storm Surges

developing storm. Winds begin to spiral faster and faster around the center of low pressure, which becomes the calm "eye" in the center of the hurricane. The hurricanes then move northwest to menace the Gulf and Caribbean coasts.

An average of eight severe storms strike the Caribbean Sea each year, and the Gulf gets even more. In 1974, Hurricane Fifi killed eight thousand people when it struck Honduras in Central America. An estimated eighteen thousand people died in 1998, most of them in Honduras, when Hurricane Mitch devastated Central America. The year 2004 was one of the most active hurricane seasons on record—during August and September alone, four large hurricanes ravaged parts of Florida and struck other areas. In 2005,

Sometimes, fierce winds around the hurricane's eye cause seawater to pile up and form a mound of water called a storm surge, which can hit ocean shores in a gigantic wave with an impact similar to a tsunami. In 1900, an unnamed hurricane hit the Gulf of Mexico coast in Texas, near the town of Galveston, which lies just off the mainland. In the hurricane's huge storm surge, waves washed right over the island. Between six thousand and eight thousand people died in what was one of the deadliest natural disasters in U.S. history.

The port of Galveston, Texas, is located on a low-lying, sandy island. The storm surge that struck in 1900 flooded the town.

Hurricane Katrina

Hurricane Katrina, which hit the United States in 2005, was the fourth largest Atlantic hurricane on record when measured by its strength. In terms of damage, it was devastating. The storm hit southern Florida on August 25 and then headed across the Gulf of Mexico toward Mississippi and Lousiana, building up strength until it hit land again on August 29. Katrina weakened as it moved inland, but it left terrible destruction at the coast. The hurricane and its record storm surges destroyed communities and took several hundred lives in Mississippi, at Bay St. Louis, Waveland, Biloxi, and Gulfport. Louisiana and Alabama were also hard hit.

The combination of storm surge and strong wind caused the levees (flood barriers) protecting New Orleans to give way the day after the hurricane. Within hours, about 80 percent of the city and several surrounding parishes were flooded with water from Lake Pontchartrain. A huge rescue effort began to help people who had not been evacuated before the storm hit. People stranded on roofs and in attics were picked up by helicopter. Several hundred people drowned or died from other, hurricane-related causes. With over one thousand deaths, one million people displaced, and untold damage to land and property, Hurricane Katrina was one of the worst humanitarian crises ever to hit the United States.

Hurricane Katrina completely destroyed homes in many communities along the Gulf of Mexico coast, including Gulfport (top). It also flooded large areas of New Orleans (middle). Thousands of evacuees from New Orleans were temporarily housed in the Astrodome in Houston, Texas (bottom), not knowing when—or if— they would be able to return home.

CHAPTER THREE

MARINE LIFE

The varied **habitats** of the Gulf of Mexico and Caribbean Sea support a huge range of plants and animals, including some species found nowhere else. Many species are closely related to those in other parts of the Atlantic. The region is also home to creatures related to Pacific Ocean species. This connection is because a channel of open water linked the Caribbean and Pacific until about 3.5 million years ago, when the isthmus of Panama rose to close the gap.

Abundance of Life

In general, marine life of all kinds is less abundant in the Caribbean than in the Gulf of Mexico. In the Caribbean, there are relatively few rivers bringing nutrients, which nourish plants that in turn feed animals. In contrast, the many rivers flowing into the Gulf of Mexico bring in large supplies of nutrients that fuel the growth of seaweeds and microscopic **algae**. These plants form the base of food chains in the region. The nutrient-rich coastal waters of the Gulf, therefore, support large stocks of fish, shellfish, and other creatures.

Coastal Habitats

Coastal habitats include sand and shell beaches, mudflats, marshes, and mangrove swamps. The Everglades is a semitropical marshland in southwestern Florida. Long

A great blue heron looks for fish in a mangrove swamp along the eastern coast of the Gulf of Mexico.

strings of barrier islands line sections of the Gulf coast, with **lagoons** and sea grass pastures between the islands and mainland. Salty pools, or *salinas*, are found on many Caribbean islands.

Coral reefs are an important habitat in the shallow waters off mainland coasts and islands. Two main types of reefs are found in the region: fringing reefs, which lie just offshore, and barrier reefs, which are found in deeper water parallel to coasts. Reefs are also found among the shallows of salt domes far out to sea in the Gulf of Mexico.

The reefs of the wider Caribbean make up 14 percent of the world's coral

Coral Reefs

Coral reefs form in warm, shallow waters in tropical and subtropical areas. These hard structures are built by small creatures called coral **polyps**. The polyps live in large colonies attached to firm surfaces, such as rocks or the reef itself. Like sea anemones, coral animals have tube-shaped bodies with a mouth on top that is surrounded by a ring of tentacles. At night, the polyps spread their tentacles to capture food. They are also nourished by tiny algae that live inside them and produce food by **photosynthesis**. The algae are nourished in turn by the polyp's waste. Natural partnerships like this are known as symbiotic relationships.

Coral polyps use minerals dissolved in seawater to build a protective, chalky skeleton around their soft bodies. When they die, their cup-shaped skeletons remain and slowly build up on top of others to form a rocky reef. The world's biggest coral reefs are thousands or even millions of years old. Scientists believe the reefs of the Florida Keys formed 125,000 years ago. Coral reefs are sometimes known as the "rain forests of the sea"—like rain forests, they support thousands of other living things, including sea anemones, sponges, sea urchins, worms, mollusks, and colorful fish.

Corals of the Caribbean and Gulf include (from left to right): *elkhorn coral, staghorn coral, pillar coral, and flower coral.*

reefs, with Puerto Rico, Hispaniola, Cuba, and the Florida Keys all having substantial reefs. The barrier reefs off Belize in Central America and the Florida Keys are home to two of the largest coral reefs in the world.

Ocean Food Chains

In the wider Caribbean, living things depend on one another for food. The relationships between plants and animals in a habitat can be shown in a food chain. Plants form the base of almost all marine food chains. Seaweeds and microscopic floating plants, or phytoplankton, use light to make their food through the process of photosynthesis. Tiny animals called zooplankton, including shrimp-like copepods, young fish, and shellfish, feed on phytoplankton. They provide food for larger creatures, such as angelfish, which in turn may be snapped up by predators at the top of the food chain, including sharks and barracudas.

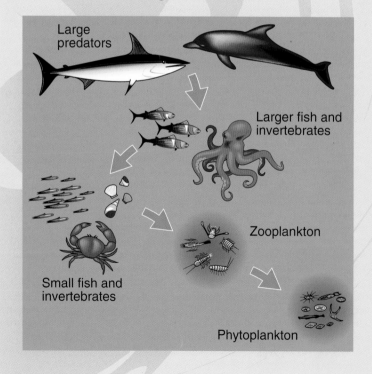

Large predators

Larger fish and invertebrates

Zooplankton

Small fish and invertebrates

Phytoplankton

The Open Sea

Many species that live in the Gulf of Mexico and Caribbean Sea inhabit open waters far from land. The open sea can be divided into several vertical layers, each of which hosts a different community of living things.

Life is most abundant in the upper waters, or **euphotic zone**, descending from the surface to 330–660 feet (100–200 m). These sunlit waters support seaweeds and plant **plankton**, which in turn feed shrimp and surface-dwelling fish. Little light reaches the **bathyal zone**, between 330–660 feet and 6,600 feet (100–200 m and 2,000 m). Without light, plants cannot grow there. Some fish and other animals seek the shelter of these gloomy waters by day and swim up toward the surface to feed at night. Most animals of the **abyssal zone**, below 6,600 feet (2,000 m), feed on scraps of food drifting down from above, or they prey on each other.

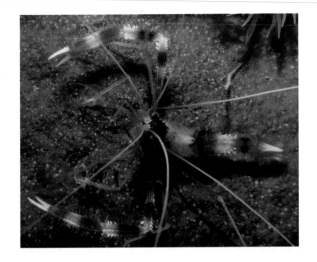

Banded coral shrimp (top) are crustaceans found on reefs in the Caribbean. The flamingo tongue snail (middle), a mollusk, has spots that help it blend in with sea fans, a type of coral that the snail eats. A moon jellyfish (bottom) floats in the waters of the Florida Keys.

as the Campeche Bank off the Yucatán Peninsula. Both sea grasses and mangroves trap drifting sediment, creating rich feeding grounds for fish, shellfish, manatees, and turtles.

Plant Life

As well as the microscopic plankton that drift at the sea surface, various types of seaweeds float in the open sea or root in the sunlit shallows close to Caribbean and Gulf shores. Coastal plants include coconut palms, which root on sandy beaches, and mangroves, which thrive in muddy **estuaries**. Sea grasses, including turtle grass, colonize the warm waters of lagoons and shallow waters offshore, such

Invertebrates

Most types of animals living in the Caribbean and Gulf of Mexico are invertebrates, creatures that lack an inner skeleton. These creatures include worms, sea urchins, mollusks (such as snails and squid), **crustaceans**, starfish, jellyfish, and sponges. The nutrient-rich waters of the Gulf support huge numbers of invertebrates. Clams, oysters, and scallops mostly live attached to the bottom, sieving small particles of food from the water. Starfish, crabs, and sea snails

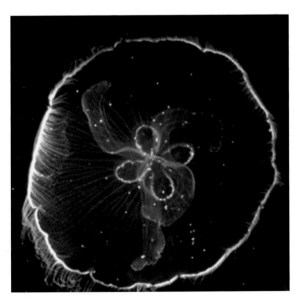

A barracuda (left) finds a meal among the many fish that inhabit coastal reefs. A peacock flounder (below) is well camouflaged on the Caribbean seafloor.

creep over rocks and reefs in search of food, while octopus and squid are more active predators.

Fish of the Caribbean and Gulf

Fish, reptiles, birds, and mammals are all vertebrates, with a bony inner skeleton. Hundreds of different fish live in the wider Caribbean. Snapper, mullet, and menhaden are among the main species targeted by fishing boats. Flying fish, tuna, and mackerel dwell at the surface, while flounders and manta rays have flattened bodies suited to life on the bottom. Sailfish and marlin are large, fast fish found in open waters. Sharks and barracudas are found there, too, and in coastal waters where they prey on reef fish.

Coral reefs are home to more types of fish than any other habitat. Parrotfish feed on the reef itself, while small fish called wrasse scavenge for scraps.

Reptiles on the Shores

Reptiles of the region include American alligators, which lurk in the swamps of the Everglades, and rare Cuban crocodiles from the marshes of Cuba. There are several types of sea turtles, including hawksbill, ridley, green, loggerhead, and leatherback turtles. Leatherbacks are the largest turtles, measuring up to 6 feet (2 m) long. Many Caribbean and Gulf turtles are now rare, partly because the beaches where they lay their eggs have been developed by humans. The endangered

Kemp's ridley turtle nests only on one beach, Rancho Nuevo in the western Gulf.

Birds

Many types of seabirds, shorebirds, and land birds frequent the wider Caribbean. Frigate birds, boobies, and tropic birds are seen far out to sea, while flamingos, spoonbills, and pelicans are common on coasts. A wide variety of land birds visit the wider Caribbean in winter. In spring, they fly hundreds of miles north to nest in Canada. Many birds follow the wide ribbon of the Mississippi as they make their annual **migration**. Caribbean islands are home to several birds found nowhere else, including the St. Vincent parrot. The Cuban hummingbird is the world's smallest bird, no larger than a bumblebee. Trinidad is known for its purple honeycreepers.

Sea and Land Mammals

Mammals of the wider Caribbean include dolphins and porpoises that live in groups known as schools. Humpback whales and northern right whales visit the region in the course of their long migrations through the oceans.

Several unique land mammals are found on the large islands of Cuba, Hispaniola, and Jamaica. The Cuban hutia is a rodent with, unusually, three stomach compartments; while the solenodon, found on Hispaniola and Cuba, look likes a hedgehog with the addition of long snout and ratlike tail.

This blue-chinned sapphire hummingbird (left) on Trinidad feeds on nectar and insects. The manatee (right) is a large, gentle plant eater. This aquatic mammal is endangered. It is threatened by motorboats, by habitat loss, and—in some regions—by hunting.

CHAPTER FOUR

PEOPLE AND SETTLEMENTS

The shores of the Caribbean Sea and Gulf of Mexico have been inhabited for thousands of years. Ancient human footprints, embedded in volcanic ash in Mexico, were identified in 2005. They indicate that people may have reached the region, including the Gulf coast, by about thirty-eight thousand years ago, which is thousands of years earlier than scientists had previously estimated.

People probably lived along Gulf and Caribbean coasts mainly because the sea offered abundant food in the form of fish and shellfish. When people learned to build boats, the relatively calm waters offered a means of transportation, both along the coast and to offshore islands. As agriculture developed in the region between 2000 and 3000 B.C., the warm climate and fertile soil of coastal plains and valleys proved good for farming beans, squash, and corn.

First Peoples

In North America, the first inhabitants of the Gulf coast lived by hunting wild animals, fishing, and gathering shellfish and plant foods. As these peoples became more settled, their societies developed into regional communities. Groups along the Gulf coast included the Calusa, of

Some parts of the Caribbean and Gulf have been farmed for more than four thousand years. In this picture, a farmer in Cuba plows a field with oxen as his ancestors would have done.

what is now Florida, and the Natchez people in the Mississippi region.

Ciboney, Taino, and Arawak peoples inhabited Caribbean coasts of South America. These groups, too, were hunter-gatherers and caught fish for food.

Ancient Cultures

Mexico's east coast was home to several advanced cultures in ancient times. The first was that of the Olmecs, who dominated the Gulf coast from about 1200 to 400 B.C. The Olmecs invented a writing system and a method of counting. Using simple tools, they carved giant stone heads that can still be seen at Tres Zapotes and La Venta today.

Far to the north, by A.D. 800, another advanced culture developed among the Eastern Woodlands people of the Lower Mississippi valley. The people of that culture became known as mound builders because of the huge earthen mounds they constructed for religious ceremonies and for the burial of their leaders.

Settling the Islands

The islands of the Caribbean have been inhabited for at least five thousand years. The Arawaks, Tainos, and other groups reached the Greater and Lesser Antilles in dugout canoes about 3000 B.C. and settled on

The Maya

Ruins of the Mayan civilization still stand at Tulum on the coast of the Yucatán Peninsula in Mexico.

From about 500 B.C., the Mayan civilization thrived in Mexico, Belize, and Guatemala. The Mayan world was divided into several kingdoms, each with its own capital and ruler. The Maya were expert architects and artists, and they built magnificent stone palaces and pyramid temples at Palenque, Chichén Itzá, and the coastal town of Tulum. They were also skilled astronomers and mathematicians, and they devised a form of writing and an accurate calendar. After A.D. 900, Mayan influence faded, and the cities of the Maya were eventually abandoned to the forests and swamps.

the islands. There, they lived by farming, fishing, and hunting. About A.D. 1300, fierce Caribs from South America raided the Lesser Antilles in canoes and settled there. The Caribs hunted, fished, gathered plants, and grew the root vegetable cassava. Carib communities still exist in the Caribbean, principally on the island of Dominica, and in South America.

The First Europeans

In the late 1400s, Europeans arrived in the wider Caribbean and changed the way of life there forever. Italian explorer Christopher Columbus sailed west across the Atlantic on a voyage sponsored by Spain. His aim was to find a new sea route to India, China, and the East Indies. Columbus landed in 1492 in the Bahamas. The Arawak people he met there guided him to Hispaniola. On later voyages, Columbus reached other Caribbean islands and the shores of Central and South America. He

Fertile Islands

"This island and all others are very fertile to a limitless degree. There are birds of many kinds, and fruits in great diversity. In the interior there are mines and metals, and the population is without number."

Christopher Columbus, impressions of Hispaniola, 1493

died believing—incorrectly—that he had found the gateway to the East, or the Indies. The Caribbean became known as the West Indies, and Europeans referred to local people as "Indians."

Expeditions and Colonies

Columbus's success inspired more Spanish expeditions to the region. From the early 1500s, Spanish adventurers came in search not only of trade routes, but of riches, such as gold and silver. The Spanish soon set up ports and **colonies** on Caribbean islands and on the shores of Mexico and Central America.

Other European powers, meanwhile, followed Spain's lead. During the 1600s and 1700s, French, English, Dutch, and Danish adventurers scrambled to lay claim to islands in the Caribbean. Many Native people were either killed or enslaved, or they died of diseases brought into the region by Europeans. France and Spain fought for control of the North American coast along the Gulf of Mexico and inland along the Mississippi River. By the 1700s, the Mississippi was in the hands of the French.

Colonists and Slaves

During the 1600s, increasing numbers of European colonists arrived to settle the region. Caribbean coasts and islands were soon divided up into large plantations growing sugar cane and tobacco, which were run by wealthy landowners. Starting in the early days of colonization,

The long colonial history of New Orleans, Louisiana, is reflected in its Creole culture, a blend of French, Spanish, and African influences. Here, the old buildings of the French Quarter—an area that survived Hurricane Katrina—are dwarfed by modern towers.

thousands of captured Africans were brought across the Atlantic to work as slaves in the plantations. They endured terrible conditions, both on the crossing and in the plantations, where they were forced to work from dawn to dusk for no wages. Caribbean slaves led several uprisings that were brutally put down by white slave owners. Throughout the 1800s, slavery was gradually abolished in the Caribbean and Gulf regions. People descended from African slaves, however, still dominate the populations of Caribbean islands today.

In the mid-1700s, French Acadians, or "Cajuns," left Nova Scotia in Canada and came to southern Louisiana. The area is still known for its Cajun heritage, including zydeco music and delicious food. During the 1700s and 1800s, every part of the wider Caribbean was controlled by one European nation or another. In the late 1800s, fresh waves of settlers arrived there from Italy and Ireland.

Caribbean Independence

During the 1900s, most parts of the wider Caribbean won full or partial independence from colonial powers. Colonial influence, however, can still be seen in the cultures of Caribbean

and Gulf nations today. The people of Martinique, colonized by France, still speak French and celebrate French holidays. Spanish influence is still clear in Mexico and on the islands of Cuba and Puerto Rico. Parts of the coast of North America along the Gulf retain a French flavor that dates back to colonial times.

Military Importance

Throughout history, the coasts and islands of the wider Caribbean have held military importance, both for local people and for distant nations. From the 1500s, the Spanish regarded Caribbean waters as their territory. This did not prevent pirates and rival nations, such as Britain, from attacking Spanish ships and seizing their rich treasures.

The 1800s saw the beginnings of U.S. interest in the region. In 1899, the United States built the first of several military bases in the Caribbean, at Guantánamo Bay in Cuba. Europeans, meanwhile, continued to defend their Caribbean interests.

In 1902, Cuba gained independence from Spain. In 1959, it became a communist nation, strongly supported by the Soviet Union. In 1962, the United States and the Soviet Union nearly went to war over the buildup of Soviet weapons on Cuba. Since that time, U.S. forces have gone into action several times to defend U.S. interests in the region, notably on the island of Grenada in 1983 and in Panama in 1989.

Growing Ports and Cities

From early times, ports and settlements grew up on bays and inlets that offered protection for shipping. Styles of architecture often reflect colonial roots. The port of Willemstad on Curaçao, with its tall buildings lining the harbor, still resembles an old Dutch port.

Havana

Havana, the capital of Cuba, was founded by the Spanish on its present site in 1519. The Spanish influence can still be seen in the cobbled squares, narrow streets, and waterfront of Old Havana and in the cathedral that dates from the 1700s. Today, modern buildings dominate the skyline in other parts of the city. Extensive docks line the much of the harbor, where Cuban sugar, citrus fruits, spirits, and minerals are exported and foreign machinery, fertilizers, and oil are brought into the nation.

Havana lies on a fine natural harbor on Cuba's northwest coast. A view along the the waterfront in Old Havana looks across to the Castillo del Morro, a fort built by the Spanish in early colonial times.

Galveston was once the biggest port in Texas. Today, its main industries include oil refining and shipbuilding.

The Gulf of Mexico has relatively few good natural harbors. Veracruz and Tampico in Mexico, however, slowly grew into major ports, along with New Orleans, Galveston, Corpus Christi, Mobile, Pensacola, and Tampa in the United States. In the Caribbean Sea, today's major ports include Havana in Cuba and Port of Spain in Trinidad.

Industrialization and Growth

In the 1800s, factories sprang up around Gulf ports, such as New Orleans, to process raw materials brought by sea and along rivers. In the 1900s, the discovery of oil and gas on land and offshore provided a boost to local industries. New Orleans is a major port in the United States, despite the fact it lies 100 miles (160 km) upriver from the Gulf itself.

Today, the nations of the wider Caribbean vary greatly, both in terms of industrialization and in standards of living. The United States is one of the world's most industrialized and wealthy nations. Other nations, including Mexico and Venezuela, are developing rapidly, while Haiti remains one of the world's poorest nations.

Survival and Challenges

A high proportion of people living around the Gulf and Caribbean still depend on the sea for their living. They harvest fish and shellfish, work on off-shore oil rigs, or find jobs in tourist hotels, restaurants, and stores. Others are farm workers, helping to raise crops—such as bananas, citrus fruit, coffee, and tobacco—that grow well on these coasts.

While the sea provides employment and sometimes wealth, it also holds dangers, including hurricanes, earthquakes, and volcanic eruptions. In 1988, Hurricane Gilbert destroyed 100,000 homes in Jamaica. Parts of Montserrat remain uninhabited following the 1995 volcanic eruption there. Many thousands of Americans along the Gulf coast lost homes to Hurricane Katrina in 2005.

CHAPTER FIVE

TRANSPORTATION AND COMMUNICATION

Vessels ranging from huge cruise ships to the smallest boats fill the harbor at St. Thomas in the Virgin Islands.

The Arawaks and other Native peoples were the first to sail the waters of the wider Caribbean, in canoes made from hollowed-out tree trunks. The term *canoe* is an Arawak word.

From Caravels to Steamboats

In the late 1400s, Europeans arrived in ships called carracks and caravels. These three- and four-masted sailing ships used a mixture of triangular and square sails that made them fast and maneuverable. A structure called a sterncastle provided quarters for the crew at the rear.

From the 1500s, Spanish galleons patrolled Caribbean waters. These ships were similar to carracks but had an extra deck for cannon to shoot at pirates and enemy warships. From the mid-1800s, ships began to be powered by steam. Paddleboat steamers ferried passengers and cargo from Gulf ports up rivers in North America.

Modern Transportation

Today in the Caribbean Sea and the Gulf of Mexico, vessels of all sizes can be seen, from small fishing boats and yachts to ferries, cruise liners, and giant **container** ships and oil **tankers**. The largest of the tankers, known as supertankers, have to tie up at deepwater moorings offshore because they are too big to dock at ports.

In the early 1900s, the first airplanes crossed the wider Caribbean. The mid-1900s saw the start of cheap flights to carry tourists to vacations on Caribbean islands. Frequent flights now link North America with the Caribbean. Sea cruises also offer a popular way to visit islands—passengers can spend their days exploring the islands and return to their ships at night. More than nine million tourists take a Caribbean cruise every year.

Cargo in the Caribbean and Gulf

Just as methods of transportation have changed over the years, so have the cargoes that vessels carry. From the early 1500s, Spanish galleons were used to ship huge quantities of gold, silver, and other riches from the Americas to Europe. An estimated $49 billion worth of treasure made its way eastward across the Atlantic between 1500 and 1820. Today, a lot of

freight goes by air, but heavy or bulky goods that can survive a longer sea voyage still travel by water. Oil and minerals, including iron ore and bauxite, go by sea. So do the less perishable crops, such as sugar, coffee, and bananas.

Pirates

Pirates flourished in the Caribbean and Gulf of Mexico from the early 1500s to the late 1700s. During this period, they gained control of the entire region and spread fear among sailors and coastal inhabitants. Some pirates attacked any ship carrying goods. Others, such as the buccaneers—most of whom were English, French, and Dutch—targeted just the Spanish. These pirates based themselves in Caribbean islands. From there, they raided Spanish coastal settlements and attacked the fleets of Spanish galleons that carried treasure from the Americas and the Caribbean islands to Europe.

This replica of a pirate ship is on show near Holetown, Barbados.

Navigation and Communication

Methods of **navigation** and communication in Caribbean and Gulf waters have changed greatly over the centuries. Early European navigators crossed the region, and other Atlantic waters, with the help of magnetic compasses. They used the position of the Sun, the Moon, and stars to calculate their **latitude**, or distance from the equator. In open water, the sailors' knowledge of waves, winds, and currents helped them navigate.

Modern ships are equipped with a variety of sensitive instruments that help sailors locate hazards, such as reefs and **shoals**, and keep track of their location. These instruments include **sonar** and radar. Ships maintain regular contact with ports, weather stations, and other vessels using radio. Modern compasses and global positioning systems (GPS) allow sailors to pinpoint their position using **satellites**.

Shipping Routes

In colonial times, Spanish ships entering the Caribbean used a channel that sailors called the Dragon's Mouth, which runs between the island of Grenada and the islands of Trinidad and Tobago. Most ships now use the Florida Straits, the Windward Passage between Hispaniola and Cuba, or the Mona Passage between Hispaniola and Puerto Rico. Once safely across these relatively shallow waters, navigation through the open waters of the seas is fairly straightforward. Shipping routes through the Gulf of Mexico and Caribbean are very heavily used. Ships in these waters may be headed for ports in the United States, Mexico, Central America, South America, the Caribbean islands, and even the Pacific Ocean.

The Panama Canal

Vessels passing between the Atlantic and Pacific Oceans sail through Caribbean and Gulf waters to reach the Panama Canal. Before 1914, all ships traveling between the two oceans had to go all the way around the southern tip of South America. Since that year, however, the Panama Canal has provided a link between the oceans through a 50-mile (80-km) channel across Panama. Thousands of miles have been cut off the journey between oceans, and more than twelve thousand vessels use the canal every year.

Salvaging Treasure

Dangers for shipping in the wider Caribbean include submerged reefs and shoals and severe storms and hurricanes. There have been wrecks there ever since ships first sailed these waters. In 1687, Captain William Phips led an early **salvage** operation. Phips' team recovered treasure from the Spanish ship *Concepción*, which sank off Cuba in 1641. Divers gulped oxygen from a weighted, air-filled barrel, a device known as a Bermuda tub.

Beginning in the mid-1900s, scuba diving and sonar have helped with undersea exploration. Scuba diving for sunken treasure off the Florida Keys became a popular activity after World War II ended in 1945.

Marine archaeologists now use a variety of sophisticated equipment to locate wrecks, including satellites, autonomous underwater vehicles (AUVs), and sonar. One spectacular find in the Caribbean Sea was the 1977 recovery of pottery and glass, gold and diamond jewelry, and many pearls from the Spanish galleon *Conde de Tolosa*, a treasure ship that sank off Hispaniola during a hurricane in 1724.

Submersibles

After a slow beginning, submarine technology advanced quickly during World War I. During the 1970s, U.S. **oceanographer** Sylvia Earle led a team of women scientists in a pioneering experiment in submarine living, which took place in the Caribbean Sea off the U.S. Virgin Islands. Earle's team spent two weeks underwater the vessel *Tektite II*. The oceanographer afterward helped develop several **submersibles**, including *Deep Flight*, which can explore ocean depths at 12,000 feet (3,660 m).

Two divers lift a wooden beam from the wreck of the Conde de Tolosa *off the coast of Hispaniola in the Caribbean Sea.*

CHAPTER SIX

RESOURCES

Natural resources of the wider Caribbean include fish, shellfish, and minerals, particularly oil and gas. Mining is causing pollution in some areas, unfortunately, which is a threat to marine life.

Commercial Fishing in the Gulf

The Gulf of Mexico is one of the richest fishing and shrimping grounds in the Americas. The shallow, nutrient-rich waters of the wide coastal shelves—such as the Campeche Bank off the Yucatán Peninsula—are especially rich in marine life. Commercial fishing boats target flounder, snapper, mullet, and menhaden among other fish. (Menhaden are often processed into fish meal for feeding farm livestock.) The region is also

Fishing Techniques

The fishing boats of the Caribbean and Gulf of Mexico target both pelagic (surface-dwelling) fish and demersal (bottom-dwelling) species. Trawl nets shaped like giant funnels are used to catch fish, including flounders and groupers, which dwell on or near the bottom. The fish swim into the net's wide mouth and get trapped in the narrow, closed end. Purse-seine nets (nets that surround and enclose fish) are used to catch surface dwellers, such as sardines, mackerel, tuna, and menhaden. Sport fishermen use fishing lines to target large, powerful species, such as marlin and barracuda.

Commercial fishing in the Gulf of Mexico: The wide mouth of a trawl net is held open by otter boards; (top) purse-seine nets used to catch menhaden are hauled in. (bottom)

An offshore fishing cage floats in front of an oil rig in the Gulf of Mexico.

prized for its shellfish, including shrimp, cupped oysters, calico scallops, crab, and lobster. The five U.S. states bordering the Gulf together net 80 percent of the nation's shrimp catch and 60 percent of the oyster catch. One-fifth of all fish caught by U.S. fishing boats are caught in the Gulf of Mexico.

Caribbean Fishing

Fish and shellfish catches are lower in the Caribbean, mainly because these waters contain fewer of the nutrients that feed the plankton at the base of the food chain. Many types of fish are found in this warm sea but in relatively small numbers. In addition, the reefs and shoals around many islands create difficulties for fishing boats. Most fish caught in the Caribbean are used to feed local people or supply tourist restaurants. Cuba, however, has a commercial fishing fleet that nets fish for foreign markets. Shellfish,

such as shrimp and lobster, are caught there, too. Demand for some species of shellfish is so high that they have been **overfished** and are now scarce.

Rich in Oil

The minerals of the Gulf of Mexico, especially oil and gas, are a major source of wealth for coastal nations. Oil mining began on land in Texas in 1901, while offshore drilling began in the 1930s. Today, more than four thousand oil rigs operate in the Gulf.

Gulf Minerals

Other minerals, including zircon, monazite, and titanium, are mined in Gulf waters. The seabed around salt domes is rich in deposits of potash, magnesium, salt, and sulfur. In the 1960s, the world's first offshore sulfur mine opened a few miles off the Louisiana coast. The state of Louisiana was soon the world's leading sulfur producer. Sulfur is mined using a method named the Frasch process. Very hot water is pumped down boreholes in the deposits. The water melts the sulfur, which is then pumped up in liquid form.

Caribbean Minerals

The Caribbean also holds valuable minerals. Titanium, chromite, and even gold have been located off Hispaniola, Cuba, and Jamaica. These minerals, however, mostly lie in water too deep for present mining methods.

Salt is a mineral that is more readily available. In Bonaire and the Bahamas, shallow, manmade basins collect seawater. When the water evaporates in the sun, it leaves the salt behind. Sand, shells, and coral are mined for use in the construction industry. **Dredging** the seabed, however, stirs up the bottom and causes harm to marine plants and coral polyps.

Energy from the Gulf and Caribbean

Oil and natural gas deposits are the remains of marine plants and animals that died millions of years ago and were later buried by layers of sediment on the seabed. Pressure and heat slowly turned the remains to oil and gas. The Gulf of Mexico and the Caribbean Sea are rich in deposits of these **fossil fuels**. The most productive areas are the waters off Louisiana, the Mexican states of Campeche and Veracruz, the island of Trinidad, and Lake Maracaibo in Venezuela. Lake Maracaibo, a large coastal inlet, holds an estimated 5 billion barrels of oil.

Hydrocarbon seeps in the Gulf of Mexico are where deposits of oil and gas rise up, or seep, through cracks in the seafloor. The seeps have unusual systems of life around them, including these 6-feet (2-m) long tube worms found in Green Canyon in the Gulf.

In the future, the wider Caribbean could also be used to produce other forms of energy. The energy of waves battering its coasts could be turned into power by wave-generating stations. The difference in temperature between warm surface water and cold bottom water could also be harnessed, using a method called ocean thermal energy conversion. Both of these techniques, however, need more development to make them cost effective.

Tourism

Tourism is a major moneymaker in the Gulf and even more so on islands of the Caribbean. Every year, over one hundred million tourists arrive from the United States, Canada, Europe, and South American nations. Vacationers come to enjoy the sunshine, blue seas, tropical vegetation, and varied cultures.

Caribbean cruises are increasingly popular, and people also enjoy yachting, sport fishing, snorkeling, and diving among the coral reefs. The construction of tourist facilities on islands—such as hotels, marinas, and airports—has to be carefully managed. Poorly sited facilities can damage coastal habitats, including mangrove swamps, reefs, and the salty pools known as *salinas*.

Vacationers relax on Seven Mile Beach on Grand Cayman Island (above). In the Caymans, tourism provides up to 70 percent of the islands' income. Many vacationers in the Caribbean scuba dive among coral reefs (below) to look at the colorful marine life, such as these squirrelfish.

CHAPTER SEVEN

ENVIRONMENT AND THE FUTURE

In the last fifty years or so, the number of people living on the shores of the Caribbean Sea and Gulf of Mexico has risen quickly. Human activities are harming the water quality, which is affecting the marine **environment**.

Pollution of Coastal Waters

One of the main problems is pollution, especially in the Gulf of Mexico, which is more heavily developed than the Caribbean. Along the Gulf, cities and towns on coasts and rivers empty **sewage** and other waste into the sea. Factories on riverbanks far inland release poisonous chemicals that end up in coastal waters. The poisons are absorbed by shrimp and other small creatures and then passed on up the food chain when shrimp are eaten by fish and people. In recent years, concerns over water quality have caused some shrimping grounds in the Gulf to close for a time.

Trash piles up at a dump on the Caribbean coast in Guadeloupe in the Lesser Antilles.

Fertilizers used on farms and plantations drain into the region's rivers. In coastal areas, these chemicals cause algae to breed quickly. The algae reduce the amount of oxygen in the water, and this process can harm fish, coral polyps, and other life forms in the Gulf of Mexico.

Dumping at Sea

Farther out to sea, dumped garbage, chemicals, and mining waste cause pollution. Oil spills are a hazard in the oilfields of the Gulf, Venezuela, and Trinidad. In 1979, an oil well named Ixtoc I blew out in the Gulf after oil and gas surging up the pipe caused a huge explosion. About 475,000 tons of crude oil gushed into the sea before the leak was sealed. Oil contaminated some 5,790 square miles (15,000 sq km) of water. Luckily, the oil slick broke up before reaching the coast, where it would have done even more damage. In addition to accidents, the steady leak of oil from wells and tankers also produces pollution.

Taking Action

Governments of coastal nations are now taking action to tackle pollution. In 1982, the United Nations drafted an agreement, the Law of the Sea, to control the disposal of waste at sea. Many Gulf and Caribbean nations signed the agreement. Some of the region's poorest nations, however, cannot afford to follow its guidelines.

A beach on Treasure Island, Florida, is polluted by an oil slick.

Changing Habitats

In the last century or so, people have made many changes to coastal habitats that have affected marine life. Marshes and other wetlands along the Gulf, for example, have been drained for farming. Lagoons, sea grass pastures, and mangrove swamps have been cleared to make way for factories, refineries, or tourist development. The courses of rivers, including the Mississippi River, have been altered, which has made the rivers drop their sediment farther out to sea. This process leads to erosion of deltas and estuaries which makes them vulnerable to flooding.

Overfishing

Stocks of some fish and shellfish, such as the queen conch and spiny lobster, are suffering because of overfishing. With the help of sonar and other modern technology, fishing and shrimping boats

A shrimper on the Texan coast of the Gulf of Mexico goes through his catch, discarding pounds of bycatch for each pound of shrimp.

now harvest such big catches that there are not enough animals left to breed. The shrimping industry affects stocks of other creatures as well as the shrimp. For every pound (0.45 kilograms) of shrimp netted, about 10 pounds (4.5 kg) of other fish and shellfish are caught. The bodies of these unwanted species, known as bycatch, are just dumped in the water.

Threats to Rare Species

Many of the region's plants, animals, and other living things are being harmed by changes to the environment. Among the species that are now scarce are animals found nowhere else in the world.

American alligators and Cuban crocodiles are both threatened by changes to wetlands. Several species of sea turtles, including Kemp's ridley turtles, are now scarce because so many have been hunted or had their habitats disturbed. The region's only unique seal, the Caribbean monk seal, has probably died out altogether because of hunting in the 1800s and more recent changes to habitats.

Global Warming

A climate change identified in recent years is affecting the world's oceans. World temperatures are slowly but steadily rising, in part because of air pollution from the burning of fossil fuels. Gases given off when these fuels burn trap the Sun's heat, producing warmer weather. The rising temperatures are warming the oceans, which makes the water expand and so raises sea levels. There are signs that land ice in polar regions is melting into the oceans because of warmer temperatures, and this could dramatically raise sea levels. Low-lying islands, such as the Cayman Islands, could disappear altogether. Scientists believe global warming increases the region's risk of severe weather—including hurricanes—and flooding. Warmer water is also harming the region's coral reefs. Many nations around the world, however, are making an effort to address global warming by reducing energy consumption and cutting down on air pollution.

Conservation of Rare Species

Some help is at hand for endangered and rare species. Tighter controls on fishing are now helping stocks of rare fish and shellfish recover. Today, conservationists are monitoring the breeding of manatees and rare turtles to make sure they do not disappear, as the monk seal did.

The best way to safeguard rare species is to protect the habitat where they live, by creating marine parks and reserves. In the Flower Garden Banks in the Gulf of Mexico, Montego Bay Marine Park in Jamaica, and the Florida Keys National Marine Sanctuary, creatures enjoy protection from hunting and other dangers. It is hoped that these refuges will help their species survive.

The Future of the Caribbean Sea and Gulf of Mexico

The Caribbean Sea and Gulf of Mexico face many challenges. Global warming may bring warmer temperatures, rising sea levels, and stormier weather to the area. If the frequency and severity of hurricanes and other storms increases, the cost—in terms of human life, the environment, and the local economies of the region—may be huge. The region, now reeling in parts from hurricane damage, is heavily dependent on its marine and coastal resources, and these are threatened by erosion, overuse, and pollution. Increases in mining, tourism, and population will put more strain on resources and the environment. Vessel

A Problem and a Plan

"Wetland loss in coastal Louisiana has reached catastrophic proportions, with current losses of 25–35 square miles (65–91 sq km) per year. Since the magnitude of the problem was identified in the 1970s, we have gained much insight into the processes that lead to wetland creation and destruction. The disappearance of Louisiana's wetlands threatens the enormous productivity of its coastal eco-systems, the economic viability of its industries, and the safety of its residents. . . . By implementing the plan's regional ecosystem strategies, it is envisioned that a sustainable ecosystem will be restored in coastal Louisiana, in large part by utilizing the same natural forces that initially built the landscape."

Coast 2050, a government coastal restoration plan to address erosion of the Louisiana coast, 1998

traffic, already heavy, will grow.

Governments are providing a framework for the future, however, with laws that control pollution and overfishing. Scientific advances, new forms of energy, and an increasing awareness of the importance of healthy seas and coastlines may help protect the Gulf of Mexico and Caribbean in the future.

TIME LINE

By 12,000 B.C. People are living along coasts of the Gulf of Mexico and Caribbean Sea.

About 3000 B.C. Arawaks and Tainos are living on Caribbean islands.

About 1200–400 B.C. Olmec people thrive on the Caribbean coast of Mexico.

About 500 B.C.–A.D. 900 Maya culture dominates the Caribbean coast of Mexico, Belize, and Guatemala.

About A.D. 800–1200 Mound builders construct burial mounds in the Mississippi valley region.

1300s Caribs from South America invade and settle on Caribbean islands.

1492 Christopher Columbus reaches Bahamas.

Early 1500s Spanish lay claim to Caribbean and Gulf coasts and islands.

Late 1500s Mass transportation of African slaves to the Americas begins.

1600s England, France, Netherlands, and Denmark lay claim to Caribbean islands.

1680s French claim Lower Mississippi region.

1718 New Orleans is founded by the French.

Mid-1700s French Acadians move to the Gulf coast from Canada.

1840s–early 1900s Settlers from Italy, Ireland, and other European countries move to the wider Caribbean.

Late 1800s Ports along Gulf of Mexico coast become industrialized.

1899 United States establishes naval base at Guantánamo Bay, Cuba.

1900 Galveston, Texas, is swamped by storm surge following a hurricane.

1901 Oil mining begins in Texas.

1902 Mount Pelée on Martinique erupts, killing more than 30,000 people.

1914 Panama Canal opens.

1933 Mining begins offshore in Gulf of Mexico.

1946 Earthquake near Hispaniola causes deadly tsunami in the Caribbean region.

1962 U.S.-Soviet hostility over weapons build up in Cuba leads to Cuban Missile Crisis.

1974 Hurricane Fifi kills 8,000 people in Honduras.

1977 Divers recover treasure from *Conde de Tolosa* shipwreck.

1979 Explosion of oil well Ixtoc I in Gulf of Mexico causes large oil slick.

1983 U.S. troops take military action on Grenada.

1988 Hurricane Gilbert destroys 100,000 homes on Jamaica.

1989 United States takes military action in Panama.

1995 Soufrière Hills volcano erupts on Montserrat.

1998 Hurricane Mitch kills an estimated 18,000 people in Central America.

2001 Kick-'em-Jenny erupts off Grenada.

2004 Four major hurricanes hit Florida in a two-month period.

2005 Hurricanes Katrina, Rita, and Wilma damage communities along the Gulf of Mexico.

GLOSSARY

abyssal zone ocean below 6,600 feet (2,000 m)

algae tiny, simple plants or plant-like organisms that grow in water or damp places

barrier island island lying parallel to the shore that protects mainland from the open ocean

bathyal zone mid-depths of ocean water between 330–660 feet deep and 6,600 feet deep (100–200 m deep and 2,000 m deep)

colony territory claimed by a nation or area occupied by settlers

condense change from gas into liquid

container large crate—used on ships, trains, and trucks—that combines many smaller pieces of freight into one shipment for efficient loading and unloading

continental drift theory that landmasses are not fixed but slowly drift across Earth's surface because of tectonic plate movement

crustacean class of animals that has an outer shell and segmented body and that includes shellfish

current regular flow of water in a certain direction

delta land composed of mud and sand deposited around the mouth of a river

dredge gather by scooping up or digging out

environment surrounding conditions in which living things exist

equator imaginary line around the middle of Earth lying an equal distance between the North Pole and South Pole

estuary area of water at a coastline where a river meets the ocean

euphotic zone upper layer of ocean water, usually defined as above 330–660 feet (100–200 m)

evaporate change from liquid into gas

evaporite mineral deposit formed on the seabed after seawater evaporates

fossil fuel coal, oil, natural gas, and other fuels formed in the ground from remains of plants or animals

freight cargo transported by sea, air, rail, or road

gulf large inlet of an ocean

habitat type of place, such as a mountain or coral reef, where plants and animals live

hydrocarbon seeps cracks found on seafloor in mineral-rich areas of bodies of water, such as the Gulf of Mexico. Hydrocarbon seeps support animals that can thrive without sunlight and oxygen, living instead on the bacteria that thrive in the mineral-rich water released by the seeps.

igneous formed from melted minerals

isthmus narrow strip of land connecting two larger landmasses

lagoon shallow area of water near a larger body of water

latitude distance north or south of the equator

low pressure atmospheric system that produces unstable, stormy weather. (High pressure produces stable weather with clear skies.) Air pressure is the weight of the atmosphere pressing down on Earth at any given point.

magma molten rock beneath the surface of Earth

mantle part of Earth between the crust and core. It is mostly solid rock, but part of it is molten.

marsh wet, usually grassy land

meteorite meteor (a piece of rock in space) that crashes onto Earth's surface

migration seasonal movement by animals from one place to another

mineral natural, non-living substance

mollusk group of animals with thin, sometimes soft shells, including clams, squid, octopus, and snails

navigation use of animal instinct or scientific skills to determine a route or steer a course on a journey

oceanographer person who studies oceans and seas

overfish catch so many fish that stocks are depleted or species made extinct

peninsula piece of land jutting out into water but connected to mainland

photosynthesis process in which plants use carbon dioxide, hydrogen, and light to produce their food

plankton microscopic plants (phytoplankton) and animals (zooplankton) that float at the surface of oceans and lakes and provide food for many larger animals

polyp small sea animal with tube-like body and tentacles that attaches to rock or other substance

prevailing wind main wind in a particular region

radar system that detects and locates objects by bouncing radio waves off them

reef chain of rock or coral or raised strip of sand in water

ridge raised area on land or on ocean bottom

salvage saving or recovering objects, such as treasure from a shipwreck

satellite vehicle that orbits Earth that can be used to send signals to Earth for communications systems; or any object in space that orbits another, larger object

sediment loose particles of rocky material, such as sand or mud

sewage dirty water from homes and factories containing chemicals and human waste

shingle deposit of small rocks, like large gravel, usually found on coastlines

shoal bank of sand just below the water surface in an ocean or sea

sonar (short for sound navigation and ranging) system that uses sound waves to measure ocean depth and detect and locate underwater objects

sounding measurement of ocean depths

spit long, narrow finger of land stretching out into water

strait water channel that connects two areas of water

subduction zone region where two tectonic plates press together, causing one to subduct, or dive below the other

submersible small underwater craft often used to explore deep parts of the ocean

subtropical in or having to do with the region of the world that borders the Tropics

tanker ship fitted with tanks for carrying liquid

tropical in or having to do with the region of the world either side of the equator between the tropic of Cancer and the tropic of Capricorn

FURTHER RESOURCES

Books

Hernandez, Romel. *Caribbean Islands: Facts and Figures*. Discovering (series). Mason Crest Publishers, 2003.

Matsen, Brad. *The Incredible Search for the Treasure Ship Atocha*. Incredible Deep-Sea Adventures (series). Enslow Publishers, 2003.

McLoone, Margo. *Women Explorers of the Oceans: Ann Davison, Eugenie Clark, Sylvia Earle, Naomi James, Tania Aebi*. Capstone Press, 1999.

Morgan, Nina. *The Caribbean and Gulf of Mexico*. Seas and Oceans (series). Raintree Steck-Vaughn, 1997.

Rhodes, Mary Jo. *Sea Turtles*. Undersea Encounters (series). Children's Press, 2005.

Vogel, Carole Garbuny. *Shifting Shores*. The Restless Sea (series). Franklin Watts, 2003.

Woodward, John. *Sunlit Zone*. Exploring the Oceans (series). Heinemann, 2004.

Web Sites

FEMA for Kids: Hurricanes
www.fema.gov/kids/hurr.htm

Florida Museum of Natural History Ichthyology Just for Kids
www.flmnh.ufl.edu/fish/Kids/kids.htm

Reef Education Network
www.reef.edu.au/

Tropical Twisters
kids.earth.nasa.gov/archive/hurricane/index.html

Volcanoes, Earthquakes, Hurricanes, Tornadoes
www.nationalgeographic.com/forcesofnature/interactive/

What's the Story on Oil Spills?
response.restoration.noaa.gov/kids/spills.html

WWF Habitats Home
www.panda.org/news_facts/education/middle_school/habitats/index.cfm

About the Author

Jen Green worked in publishing for fifteen years. She is now a full-time author and has written more than 150 books for children about natural history, geography, the environment, history, and other topics.

INDEX